W9-BEJ-176

THE WHOLE OF BRUSSELS

AND ITS SURROUNDINGS

Text, photographs, design, lay-out and printing, entirely created by the technical department of EDITORIAL ESCUDO DE ORO, S.A.

Rights of total or partial reproduction and translation reserved.

Copyright of this edition for photographs and text: © EDITORIAL ESCUDO DE ORO, S.A. - Palaudarias, 26 - 08004 Barcelona (Spain).

8th Edition, May 1995

I.S.B.N. 84-378-0986-X

Dep. Legal B. 22334-1995

SALE DISTRIBUTOR : Editions A.V.M. n.v.
Marconistraat 5 (Industriepark) B-8400 OOSTENDE
Tel.: (059) 70.86.22 - Fax.: (059) 70.10.53

Engraved panorama of Brussels printed by Martin de Tailly in 1639. A re-print of 1748 is shown in the Broodhuis.

PREFACE

Brussels, the city of contrasts! Coveted by some, disputed by others. A French language "oasis" in Flemish country. An historical symbol of a continuous struggle against oppression. It is also a lovable town — which may explain why it is heart-shaped like all the towns in Brabant. Brussels, although a thousand years old, has been obliged, at the end of the Second World War, to adapt itself to the whirling evolution of housing and above all the unstoppable increase in motor traffic. Everyone regrets that this modern development has not always taken place within the bounds of good taste, but nevertheless the capital of Europe has much to offer to those who are convinced that beauty is not confined to Sienna, Toledo or Rhodes.

A visit to Brussels begins traditionally in the Grote Markt. This "forum" has very frequently formed the historical centre of the town. The struggle for in-

Brussels is still a lively town in spite of being a thousand. It has a double aspect: old and modern. A town of memories.
Formidable architecture. An art centre on a world scale. Fascinating history full of love, violence and passion.

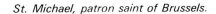

St. Michael, patron saint of Brussels.

dependence, the foundation of the gilds, the appointment of rulers and judges, tournaments and joisting all began in the place entitled ''the most beautiful forum in the world'' by Jean Cocteau.

Brussels is not an ''ancient'' town. It developed on an island surrounded by marshes nourished by the stream, the Zenne, which in the past, has caused quite a lot of emotion by flooding. It now flows, unseen, under the town. The island which was called Sint-Gorikseiland, after the Bishop of Cambrai and Arras, possessed the first landing-stage in the ninth century, the first on the Zenne. A harbour was later constructed there. The creation of a fortified stronghold on the island led to the development of a small agglomeration of soldiers, merchants and officials. Devotion to Saint Goedele, who together with Saint Michael, is patroness of the town was a unifying factor in religious matters.

This primitive settlement developed fast especially on the hill on the island where there was a chapel dedicated to the Archangel Michael, who can be observed slaughtering the Devil on the city's coat-of-arms. This chapel was changed in 1047 into the Collegiate church of Saint Michael and Saint Goedele. A few years ago poor Saint Goedele was unmercifully liquidated by ecclesiastical reformers and the church became the Cathedral of Saint Michael. This beautiful building is the most glorious example of the Brabant gothic style. During a guided visit the various styles ranging from the thirteenth century romanesque to the late decorated of the sixteenth will be pointed out. The Cathedral possesses many works of art, including the chapel of the Sacrament which is illumined by the splendid renaissance-inspired stained glass windows by Barend van Orley. They were a gift from the brothers and sisters of the Emperor Charles V.

The town hall of Brussels.

Everyone talking about Brussels thinks in the first place of the Grote Markt, the heart of the town's constant renewal. Just like the Agora in Athens, and the Roman Forum, it too has played an important part in the history of Brussels. Economic life developed round it. The first houses were built by merchants, who were followed by the gilds. A town hall was constructed there in 1402. It was started by James van Thienen. Charles the Bold laid the foundation stone of the right wing in 1444. John van Ruysbroek was nominated architect of the tower in 1449. The decorative master-piece of the statue of St. Michael, by Martin van Rode, was placed on the top in 1465. This gothic construction is particularly important for its exterior decoration which includes the most outstanding examples of fourteenth and fifteenth century sculpture from Brussels. The back of the building, bounded by the Vruntstraat and the Guldenhoofdstraat, was built between 1708 and 1717 in Louis XIV style by Cornelius van Nerven. This site has previously been occupied by the Cloth Hall, built in 1353, but completely destroyed during the shelling of Brussels by Marshal de Villeroy in 1695, on Louis XIV's orders.

The interior of the town hall is very varied and luxurious. It is worth a visit for the collection of sixteenth, seventeenth and eighteenth century tapestries alone. Both architecture and collections make the capital's town hall one of the most remarkable of European monuments.

Directly opposite there is another historical building: the Broodhuis (Bread-house). The previous thirteenth century Broodhuis was built in wood. It was reconstructed for the first time in 1404, but its original purpose was given up.

The duke of Brabant made it into the Chamber of

The town hall tower is at least 96 m. high.

The Broodhuis in its beautiful medieval decor.

Tolls, the Court of Forestry and the offices of the General Receiver of Brabant. It received the new name of "Duke's House".

Entirely rebuilt between 1515 and 1530 under Charles V it became known as the "King's House" which referred to his title of King of Spain. The new gothic building was created by such architects as A. Keldermans, L. van Bodeghem and above all, H. van Pede. It was severely damaged in 1695 by the above mentioned shelling by de Villeroy. It was rebuilt and more or less mutilated in 1763, but Brussels bought it in 1872. It looked frightful and was therefore completely demolished between 1873 and 1885 and rebuilt by the city architect, Victor Jamaer. He drew his inspiration

from old engravings and the town hall of Oudenaarde which had been built in the sixteenth century by Henry van Pede. The city council decided on March 3, 1860 to erect a monument to Egmont and Hoorn directly in front of the Broodhuis, which occurred in 1864. Fifteen years later it was removed to the Kleine Zavel Park. The Broodhuis has been a town museum since 1887. It contains a rich fund of documents about the folklore and local as well as more general history and archaeology of the capital. In addition, interesting collections of pottery, porcelain and lace… and the huge wardrobe of about three-hundred and fifty costumes of Mannekenpis.

A daily flower-market takes place in this attractive

The flower-market brightens the "most beautiful forum in the world" every day.

decor of medieval gild-halls. Three very attractive façades in Italian baroque style with a typical Flemish touch may not be missed. The row illustrated here between the Guldenhoofdstraat and the Boterstraat, begins with "De Vos" (The Fox) which was the property of the Sellers of thread and ribbons in the fourteenth century. After the shelling of 1695 rebuilt in 1699 with on top of the façade the statue of St. Nicholas. Next door rises the strange gable top of "De Hoorn" (The Horn) or Boatmen's House. It copies the stern of a seventeenth century ship. "De Wolvin" (The She-wolf) or House of the Archers, (see the detail in the photograph) bears a bas-relief of

Romulus and Remus as well as symbolic sculptures of Truth, Falsity, Peace and Discord. Roman emperors are depicted in the medallions and at the very top the Phoenix as a souvenir of the three fires which had damaged the house. The following house "De Zak" (The Sack) or House of the Coopers and Carpenters, was their meeting place. The façade is decorated with the tools of their trades. Number 3 bears the names "De Cruywagen" (The Wheelbarrow), or the "Vettewariërs" (Candlemakers) and was restored by the traders in oil and candles after the 1695 shelling. At its top is a niche for the statue of their patron, Saint Gillis. The corner-house (see detail) is called the

All the façades in the Grote Markt are architectural wonders: "de Koning van Spanje" (King of Spain) with its proud octagonal dome surmounted by "Faam" (Fame) with its banderole; "de Wolvin" (she-wolf) or "Het huis van de Boogschutters" (Archers' House) with the sun-god Phoebus crowning the pediment; the six houses included in the majestic "Huis van de Hertogen van Brabant" (House of the dukes of Brabant) which is like an Italian palace.

The Grote Markt swims in a sea of light during special festivities such as when the famous "Omme-gang" (Procession) shines and glitters in the fairy-like medieval scene.

Beautiful names for beautiful houses. ''Het Ammanskamerke'' (The judge's little house), ''De Duif'' (The Dove) where Victor Hugo lived in exile, ''De Gulden Boot'' (The Golden Boat) with its statue of the bishop of Brussels, Boniface; ''Den Engel'' (The Angel), ''Anna'', ''Jozef'' and ''Den Hert'' (The Deer), provide the visitor with unforgettable memories when they are decorated with the colourful flags of the ''Ommegang'' procession.

Two objects typical of Brussels: the memorial tablet to the freedom fighter Evrard 't Serclaes with the connected motto of "the caress of the arm" and the legendary Mannekenpis who at the corner of the Stoofstraat and the Eikstraat watches the daily pilgrimage of tourists pass by.

"Koning van Spanje" (King of Spain) or "Bakkers-huis" (Bakers' house). This remarkable house has an octagonal dome and six symbolical figures of Power, Grain, Wind, Fire, Water and Providence decorate the cornice. The façade bears medallions of the Roman emperors. Between the Heuvelstraat and the Hoedenmakersstraat, the broad front of the seventeenth century "Huis van de Hertogen van Brabant" (House of the dukes of Brabant) appears.

On the corner of the Hoedenmakersstraat stands "De Berg van Thabor" (Mount Thabor), beside "De Roos" (The Rose) and then the impressive "Brouwershuis" (Brewers' Hall), which was previously called "De Gulden Boom" (The Golden Tree). A private Brewing museum is conserved in its cellar. House number 9 is called "De Zwaan" (The Swan) where in 1885 the Belgian Workers' Party, later to become the Socialist Party, was founded about forty years after Karl Marx and Friedrich Engels had met there. The oldest of the group is number 8, "De Sterre" (The Star), where the town reeve lived in the fourteenth century. From the balcony he watched executions in the Grote Markt. Evrard 't Serclaes, the hero was "murdered in a cowardly way for his defence of the rights of the town" there on March 31, 1388. A memorial plaque to the Burgomaster K. Buls and to 't Serclaes has been placed in the gallery. According to the legend anyone who touches Evrard's arm will be happy for a year and if it is a girl, she will marry within the year.

Brussels' oldest and most noteworthy citizen is obviously the legendary Mannekenpis. The ever increasing crowd of tourists who daily visit the corner of the Stoofstraat and the Eikstraat underlines the growing popularity of the "little fellow" as the rogue is often called by shy Japanese girls. Nothing is known about

He is certainly the most popular "citizen" of the capital. His wardrobe — which can be visited in the Broodhuis — consists at the moment of at least three-hundred and fifty different costumes.

The centre of the town has begun lately to look quite different. Only a wide road remains of the former Brouckèreplein, the solid Beursgebouw (Exchange) looks over an area of modern planning, the Nieuwstraat has become a pedestrian shopping precinct with a luxurious roofed-in centre called "City 2".

Who can remember the Noordstation on the site now occupied by the high-rise Rogier Centre?

his origins. The sculptor Jeremy Duquesnoy was commissioned in 1619 by the city council to make a statue to decorate the source called the ''Juliaenkensborre''. This marked the birth of Mannekenpis and the stories about him would never stop increasing. He has already had many adventures. He has been torn off his pedestal and stolen, but the thieves have always been firmly dealt with. He has received, because of his reputation, many native and foreign decorations. He received his first official costume in 1698 from Maximilian of Bavaria and from that moment onwards his wardrobe contained about three-hundred and fifty different suits which vary from military uniform to all sorts of sports clothes. He

wears his marquis' outfit each year at the opening of the Brussels' Fair and he puts on a soldier's uniform for July 21st. To celebrate the liberation by the allies he wears the dress uniform of the Welsh Guards on September 3 and on the next day the battle-dress of the Piron brigade. Hè has been photographed more often than anyone else in Brussels.

The Exchange in the Anspachlaan was built between 1871 and 1873 in neo-baroque style to plans by Leon Suys. Six heavy Corinthian columns support the entablature which bears a triangular pediment containing Jacquet's bas-relief of Belgium, with its Industry and Marine.

The Nieuwstraat is one of the busiest streets in the

The memorial in the Martelarenplein to the dead who fell during the revolution of 1830.

The historic Muntplein has been given a new function as the centre, of the well-known festivities called the ''Mallemunt''.

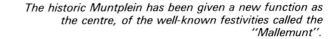

Every passer-by's attention is caught by the typical style of the Koninklijke Vlaamse Schouwburg (Royal Flemish Theatre) in the Lakensestraat.

This is not a picture of the glamorous south, but of the popular restaurants in the heart of Brussels.

lower town. It runs parallel to Brouckèreplein and Adolf Maxlaan, leading at one end to the Muntplein and at the other the Rogierplein, which is dominated by the skyscrapers of the Sheraton Hotel and the Rogier Centre. This Centre contains almost throughout the year various exhibitions and trade fairs, as well as two theatres of which one is the "Théâtre National". "City 2", a luxuriously built covered shopping centre containing not only ultra modern boutiques but food shops and department stores can be reached via the Nieuwstraat and Rogierplein. The Muntschouwburg on the Muntplein was opened by the production of "La Caravane du Caire" by Grétry on May 25, 1819. The revolution of 1830, which led to Belgian independence, broke out after a performance of Auber's "La muette de Portici". The same theatre became world famous with the creation of Maurice Béjart's "Twentieth Century Ballet" and in recent years its director Gerard Mortier has infused new life into opera there. The Muntplein, which is a pedestrian precinct, forms a successful entertainment centre with "Mallemunt" in the summer. There has long been discussion about the restoration of the remarkable buildings round the Martelarenplein. In the meantime it shelters the war memorial to the dead of 1830. The Royal Flemish Theatre, in the Lakensestraat, is remarkable in style: a mixture of Flemish renaissance, Brabant late renaissance and... Indian temple architecture. The original building dates from 1887. It was seriously damaged by fire in 1955, and subsequently restored and renewed inside.

At Brussels' heart is the restaurant centre of the "Ilôt Sacré", which is also very attractive for a stroll. The architect Jan-Pieter Cluysenaer led the building of the Saint Hubert Gallery between 1846 and 1847, which is

The "Ilôt Sacré" is worth a stroll for its architecture as well.

The majestic Saint Hubert galleries are the oldest covered streets in Europe.

a continuation of the Queen's and King's Galleries. It is 1200 m. long. The claim has been made that is was the first covered shopping street in Europe. It is still busy because of its theatre, cinema, restaurants and good shops.

A pause at the new fountain at the bottom of the Bergstraat affords a good view of the well-restored stepped gables before you.

The Congreszuil (Pillar of Congress) was erected between 1850 and 1859 by the architect Joseph Poelaert as a memorial to the National Congress which after 1830 created the Belgian Constitution. Leopold I posed the first stone of this 47 metre high pillar in 1850 and his statue, as first King of the Belgians, tops it.

The platform gives a splendid view over the lower parts of the town. A symbolical representation of the freedoms assured by the constitution: freedom of worship (front, left) by Simonis, freedom of association (right), by Fraikin, freedom of the press (Lignestraat side) and freedom of education, both by Geefs, decorate its plinth.

On November 22, 1922, King Albert I presided over a moving ceremony during which the remains of the unknown soldier were placed here. From then onwards a ceremony has taken place every year on November 11, in the presence of the royal family. Behind the Pillar of Congress rise the majority of government offices.

The Herb Garden has been obliged to give up half its ground for the construction of the road tunnel which starts at the Rogierplein. At the top of the garden the Forestry Museum houses an extensive collection of vegetable oils and types of wood. A specialized library in the Herbarium contains examples of dried plants from all over the world.

The Warande, or Brussels' Park, lies between the Royal Palace and the Parliament buildings. It was created in 1787 by Joachim Zinner and is 26 acres in area. It is completely symmetrical. The walks are decorated with pleasing statues and the two lakes give children a chance to sail their boats.

The Parliament Building, or Palace of the Nation, was completed in 1783. It was then occupied by the Sovereign Council of Brabant which had judicial, political and law giving powers. It was removed at the end of the "Ancien Régime". The Transitional Government after the revolution of 1830 met in the same building and it received its present function at

The attractively restored step gables of the Bergstraat.

The Pillar of Congress.

the first sitting of the National Congress in the same year. The chamber for the Senate was only ready in 1850.

The front was planned by the architect Godecharle: eight modern Ionic columns support a pediment with a bas-relief depicting "justice rewarding virtue and punishing vice".

At the further side of the park stands the Royal Palace. The building consisted at the end of the eighteenth century of two pavilions divided by a street which prolonged the central lane in the park. King William I of the Netherlands joined the two buildings by a gallery. Leopold II initiated the construction of the present Royal Palace (1904-1910) in Louis XVI style to plans by the architect Henry Maquet. There is a bas-relief by T. Vinçotte on the pediment depicting Belgium between Agriculture and Industry, with in the left corner, a symbolical representation of the River Maas and in the right, of the River Scheldt.

The central building is connected by galleries and small constructions to two pavilions: on the left that of the Civil List (the ruler's official income) and on the right Bell-Vue house where i.a. Prince Leopold and Princess Astrid lived after their marriage in 1926. To the left of the staircase of honour on the first floor is the Empire Room, the Small White, and the Large White Drawing Rooms. To the right the Thinker's Room, the Great Gallery (41 m. long and 10 m. wide) which leads to the Throne Room and further to the Marble Hall. In the left wing are the King's apartments, with to the right accomodation for visiting heads of state. The ruler gives audience in the Large White Drawing Room with its beautiful tapestries, of which the furniture comes from the Tuileries Palace. The Great Gallery is one of the most attractive apartments in the palace, furnished as it is with work by

The remains of the Unknown Soldier which have rested between these two lions since November 11, 1922.

The Kruidtuin (Herb Garden) was planned in 1826 by the Royal Society of Agriculture. Statues by famous artists such as C. Meunier, K. van de Stappen and J. Dillens stand in front of the buildings. The city park stretches between Parliament, the Royal Palace and the Academy, and is a grand opportunity for a walk for every citizen of Brussels.

The Royal Palace in Brussels.

the architect Balat in Louis XVI style. The King's study is on the ground floor facing an inside court-yard. The Royal Palace can be visited annually, free, during July.

The present day Koningsplein was planned by Charles of Lorraine, who governed the Austrian Netherlands at the end of the eighteenth century. On the hill on which stood the attractive castle of the dukes of Bra-bant which was devastated by fire in 1731, this popular Governor developed a new district. It includ-ed the Koningsplein, Paleizenplein, the City park and neighbouring streets. The new square where the so-called ''Baliën van 't Hof'' had stood, was conceived in neo-classical style. The French architect Guimard was inspired by the Stanislas Square in Nancy. In the symmetrical centre rose, at one time, the bronze statue of Charles of Lorraine (1794). It was destroyed during the French Revolution by the Sansculottes and replaced by the Tree of Liberty. This was cut down in 1815. It was replaced in 1849 by the statue of the crusader and King of Jerusalem Geoffrey of Bouillon. The church of Saint James on the Koudenberg (1776) built in pure neo-classical style, lost its original character when a hexagonal tower and dome were added in 1849 by the architect Suys. The front im-itates a Roman temple, and is the royal family's parish church. One of the seven hills on which Brussels is built, is called the Hofberg, near the Central station.

The Great Gallery in the Royal Palace.

△

The Throne Room.
After the abdication of
King Leopold III in
favour of his son
Boudewijn on July 16,
1951, in the Ball
Room, its name was
changed to Throne
Room.

◁

The Empire Room was
the first Palace ball
room.

The Small White Drawing Room.

The King gives audience to foreign statesmen in the Large White Drawing Room with its marvellous tapestries.

The church of Saint James on the Koudenberg (St.-Jacob-op-de-Koudenberg) and the statue of Geoffrey of Bouillon.

The gardens of the Library which form part of the Albertina complex.

The noble Ravenstein House from the Burgundian period.

From the steps of the Albertina complex the knightly statue of King Albert, by the sculptor Alfred Courtens, the white statue of Queen Elizabeth after Cliquet, the slim towers of the town hall, and the attractive façades of the Magdalenastraat can be observed.

To the right, at the back, stands Ravenstein House, which is the only noble home from the Burgundian period which remains. It was bought by the town in 1896 and well restored by Paul Saintenoy. Above the arcade leading to the Keizerslaan there is a large stone sundial with twelve niches containing a clock and a carillon of twenty-three bells. Peter Benoit's Chime Song and Grétry's "Waar kunnen we beter zijn" (where could be better than here?) are played at the quarters. Belgian historical figures dance in the niches on the hour. On the roof top a Jaquenart dressed in the Brussels' costume of 1830 strikes with his stick a bell weighing 1.750 kg.

The corner of the Kleine Zavel was planned by the architect Beyaert, with its statue of Egmont and Hoorn surrounded by those of William the Silent by Lodewijk van Bodeghem, Hendrik van Brederode by the sculptor Cornelius de Vriendt, of the botanist Rombaut Dodoens, Mercator, the burgomaster Jan van Locquenghien, the painter Barend van Orley, the geographer Ortelius, and Marnix van St. Aldegonde. The Zavel district is dominated by the Egmont Palace which in a shocking condition was sold by the town to the State in 1964 and then passed on to the Foreign Office. It has been completely restored and is the scene of important government receptions and international conferences.

The Hallepoort is the last remains of the second ring of town walls. It was restored and rebuilt by the ar-

The statue of the counts Egmont and Hoorn on the Kleine Zavel.

The inside courtyard of the Egmont Palace.

The impressive Law Courts were built in 1866 by the architect Poelaert who was inspired by Greek classical art. It covers about 26.000 m^2 or 4.000 m^2 more than St. Peter's in Rome. The dome is 103 m. high and affords a splendid view of the town.

The Hallepoort.

The Steenpoort with its old watch-tower called the Rollebeektoren in the Keizerslaan.

chitect Beyaert in 1868 as a keep and houses the Museum of Weapons and Armour.

The so-called Anneessens Gate in which the magistrate Anneessens was imprisoned formed part of the eleventh century town wall. The architectural value of St. Michael's Cathedral and its treasures has already been described.

Work on it continued for three centuries, from the thirteenth to the sixteenth. Its variety of architectural styles is not, therefore, surprising: from early gothic, via romanesque, and from high and late gothic to baroque. Building was begun in 1226 on orders from

Henry I, Duke of Brabant. Beginning with the choir pillars which were finished about 1250 and are in romanesque-gothic style while the early gothic choir was completed in 1280 and the Maes chapel in 1665 in renaissance style on the order of J.B. Maes, a Knight of St. James. It is possible here only to give a few indications which will encourage those interested to see for themselves: for example the subtle play of pure lines which can be observed from the middle of the transept. Each stained glass window is a unique separate work of art by Barend van Orley. The neo-gothic high altar in gilded copper is decorated with

The romanesque-gothic Cathedral of St. Michael, the most important and impressive church in the capital. Building took three centuries — from the thirteenth to the sixteenth.

The first stone of the chapel of the Holy Sacrament was laid in 1334 and it was finished in 1540. It is a fine example of late gothic church architecture.

The rich interior of St. Michael's Cathedral.

symbolical figures. Three chapels, of the Holy Sacrament, Saint Mary Magdalene or Maes chapel, and the Lady chapel open onto the choir ambulatory. They are illuminated by four romanesque-gothic windows with stained glass by Capronnier (1840) to designs by Navez. Roger Van der Weyden (1464) and Frans Van den Stock (1495) who were both Brussels' town painters, are buried near the chapel of the Holy Sacrament. The remarkable pulpit (1699) was made by the well-known Verbruggen of Antwerp. The Cathedral possesses a Brussels' lace work of Our Lady, seventeenth century chalices, the sceptre (seventeenth century) which belonged to the Archduchess Isabelle, Archduke Albert's sword, and a golden monstrance (17 kg.) which was the gift of the family Arenberg in 1837. The oldest and most valuable treasure is the reliquary of the Cross in wood and silver dating from about the year 1000 and engraved with the artist's name, Drahmal.

The Magdalene chapel, on the street of the same name, is almost entirely gothic in style with an eighteenth century baroque entrance. The former chapel of St. Anne in the Bergstraat was built onto the side of the Magdalene chapel in 1958. They complement each other and form a remarkable whole.

The romanesque part of the Kapelle church in the Kapellestraat makes it one of the most interesting in the country. A chapel was founded in this densely populated part of Brussels in 1134 and became, in 1210, a parish church. It was closed to Catholics twice: in 1579 when it was used by the Protestants and in 1797 during the French Revolution. In 1803 it was reopened as a parish church and in 1860 thoroughly restored by the architect Jamaer.

The six side chapels contain interesting objects including seventeenth century carved confessionals by P.D. Plumier and fifteenth century frescoes. In the third chapel lie the graves of Peter Bruegel the Elder and his wife Marie Coucke. A memorial slab in the large chapel recalls Frans Anneessens, head of the Gilds of Brussels, and fighter for independence who was beheaded in the Grote Markt in 1719.

The Zavel church stands between the Grote Zavel and the Kleine Zavel gardens. A chapel to Our Lady was founded there in 1304. The legend, depicted on an extremely beautiful sixteenth century Brussels' tapestry shows how the saintly Beatrice Soetkens, from Antwerp, stole a statue of Our Lady from the cathedral in Antwerp and took it by boat along the Scheldt and the Zenne to Brussels. She arrived close by the range belonging to the crossbowmen of Brussels and they took the statue under their protection. A procession was later organized and even the duke of Brabant and his eldest son carried the miraculous figure. This is at the origin of the famous Brussels' "Ommegang" (Procession) which happens with great pomp every year on the first Thursday of July.

The Zavel church is the best late gothic church in Belgium and was built during the Burgundian period. One of its peculiarities is the possession of five aisles. The sacristy behind the attractive choir dates from 1549 and is a remarkable example of richly decorated architecture. The choir is large and full of the light from the fourteen metre high stained glass windows.

The gothic chapel of the Holy Virgin was added to St. Michael's Cathedral in 1653 at the desire of the Grand Duchess Isabelle.

This chapel in fact belonged to the Gild of Crossbowmen and is a master-piece of the complete harmony of pure line. The magnificent rose window in the outer wall of the right hand transept is a unique example of late gothic decoration.

In the old town centre near Sint-Gorikseiland, in the Rijkeklarenstraat, stands the church of the Rich Clares. This order was founded in 1212 by St. Francis

The chapels of Mary Magdalene and St. Anne were combined successfully in 1958.

and St. Clare, and is a community of contemplative nuns. St. Clare came from a noble family and under St. Francis' influence she forsook her home, put on the poor habit and took her vows. This was the basis of the Second order of the Sisters of St. Clare, which aimed at a strict life of extreme poverty.

Near the Zuidstraat in the Kolenmarkt stands the church of Our Lady of Mercy (O.-L.-Vrouw van Goede Bijstand). It was already mentioned in the twelfth century but only became important in 1625 when a shoemaker called Jacob Meeus, discovered a statue of the Blessed Virgin to which miraculous powers were attributed. It was honoured from then

onwards as Our Lady of Mercy. The building was damaged by destruction and fire and restored in 1825 to commemorate the statue's two-hundred years of existence. The baroque façade was restored between 1847 and 1849 and from 1910 a copy of the statue has been kept in a niche while the real oaken statue is in the Broodhuis. The church interior is reminiscent of the seventeenth century Italian renaissance with a high altar partly in marble and wood from a drawing by Peter van Baurscheit of 1701.

The Sisters of St. Clare resided from 1343 onwards near the Hallepoort. When their convent was burned down by Calvinists in 1588 they were given permis-

The Zavel church is made particularly fine by its skilfully carved ornamentation.

sion to take over the old, deserted monastery of Nazareth near the Sint-Gorik church. After various adaptations and rebuilding, as for example after the shelling of 1695, the convent was closed in 1796. In 1806 it was again opened to the faithful and the left and right aisles were added in 1824 and 1833 respectively by order of the Brussels Town Council. The original Spanish brick-work was revealed by restoration work in 1954 and the façade has regained its original warm colour.

The church has inside the form of a Latin cross. Ionic columns which are well painted as imitation marble, support the roof. The black and white marble tops are ornamented with angels' heads. On a socle, above the high altar, stands a stone of Our Lady of the Immaculate Conception. To right and left are eighteenth century painted wooden statues of St. Peter and St. Paul. The oak pulpit in Louis XIV style comes from the chapel of the Holy Cross (H. Kruiskapel). Five confessionals of about 1700 adorn the walls.

Not far distant stands the Katelijne church, in the Oude Graanmarkt. The St. Katelijne dock was filled in after the flooding of the Zenne in 1850 and the present church built there to plans by the architect Poelaert. The duke and duchess of Brabant laid the first stone on September 25, 1854. The architect was

A glance into the impressive proportions of the Zavel church shows why it took a century to build.

apparently aiming at originality and mixed various styles without getting them to harmonize:
a bit of renaissance and a bit of baroque. Experts claim there to be a lack of proportion in the separat parts and especially the façades.

The church has nevertheless architectural value because it marked a nineteenth century attempt at renewal. The old tower stands to the right of the present church and is the only remains from before the demolition of 1893. It is rumoured that the church cannot stand long because of the poor quality of the building materials. The white sand-stone of which it

consists seems not to be able to resist a damp climate. The church of the Beguines, in the Begijn-hofplein, is in the same area. It is the most important baroque church in Brussels. The first beguines in Brussels received permission from John I, Duke of Brabant, round 1250 to live in community. They built their home in a swampy meadow crossed by ditches. Their beguinage was given the name of Our Lady of the Vineyard, and became so successful that it counted twelve-hundred members. A beautiful gothic church built in the fourteenth century shows that there was no lack of money. The religious wars

spelled the end of this prosperity. The beguinage was plundered and destroyed and in 1584 the church was sold and demolished. The first stone of the present church was only laid in 1657 and it was finished in 1676. Decay set in at the end of the seventeenth century. The beguinage lost its original purpose and became a home for prosperous ladies. The community was disbanded at the French Revolution and its possessions confiscated. The town of Brussels became the official owner in 1839 while in 1883 the last beguine in Brussels died. The builder of the most attractive of Beguine churches is uncertain. Luc Faid'herbe of Malines, a pupil of Rubens, has been claimed to be the architect. Its façade is in any case one of the most beautiful in the country and a very rich example of Italo-Flemish baroque. It is worth going inside. The interior is a mixture of baroque and gothic with a high altar in black and white marble made by the sculptor van Mons for the abbey church of Kortenberg. It was transferred to the beguinage in 1803 when the abbey closed. In the Nieuwstraat, the commercial heart of Brussels, among high-rise department stores, is the Finisterrae church.

This area was peaceful and sparsely populated in the middle ages. A gothic chapel with the peculiar name "Venstersterre" was built there in the fifteenth century. It became a parish church in 1646 as the area became more populated but the present building was only finished in 1730. The builder is unknown — perhaps best as his creation has little architectural value. Inside it is ore important.

Attention is drawn by an attractive white marble altar of 1853. The choir stalls in Louis XIV style are attributed to J.B. van der Haeghen, a picture by Kasper de Crayer and a decorative pulpit are all impressive. Among the churches in the capital, St. Nicholas' near

In the third chapel of the six in the side aisle of the Kapelle church stands the funeral slab of Peter Bruegel and his wife.

the Beursgebouw (Exchange) occupies a special place. It belongs, as it were, to the holders of market stalls, and shop-keepers. This gothic church dates from the fourteenth and fifteenth centuries, and has suffered greatly from plundering and destruction. The successful restoration was completed in 1956. The interior is remarkable: beautiful oaken Louis XVI panelling and pulpit in the same style, and an attractive wrought iron gate enclosing the choir. The high altar created by Cornelius van Nerven is impressive because of its high Corinthian columns supporting the entablature and its attractive king's cloak. The

reliquary of the Gorkum Martyrs in gilded copper was made in 1868 by Höllner, and is one of the church's most valuable possessions. When describing the Kapelle church, nothing was said — on purpose — about the nearby Brigittinen church. So many typical corners of Brussels have fallen to the demolition hammers and been replaced by skyscrapers, that when something manages to escape there is reason for jubilation — which is just what has happened to the skilfully restored — in 1965 — baroque façade of the former Brigittinen church. Archduchess Isabelle gave permission in 1623 to the order of Saint Bridget, a

The oaken pulpit in the Kapelle church depicts Elijah's flight into the cave to escape the wrath of Jezebel. His food is brought by an angel.

The church of Our Lady of Mercy (O.L.-Vrouw van Goede Bijstand) is reminiscent of a seventeenth century renaissance building.

fourteenth century Swedish saint who founded the Brigittines, to settle in the centre of Brussels. The church was consecrated in 1667 by Monseigneur Crucis, archbishop of Malines. The Emperor Joseph II disbanded the order in 1784 and the church became a library and subsequently served various other purposes. The old meeting place of the crossbowmen the ''Groot Koninklijk en Nobel Serment'' founded in 1201, was behind the church until the idiotic rage to demolish everything. It was one of Brussels' oldest inns, surrounded by a charming garden and with an old bowling alley, where one could meet anyone from an important civil servant to a local stall-holder in the shadow of two legendary trees. Important Flemish figures such as Herman Teirlinck and August Vermeylen often came there for a pint and a game of dice. Oh, for the good, old days...

Nearby is the Miniemen church. Also known as the church of St. John and St. Stephen, it shows the transition from the seventeenth century Flemish baroque to eighteenth century neo-classicism. It is remarkably pure in style. The begging order of the Miniemen, founded by St. Francis of Paula in 1474, were given permission by Albert and Isabelle to move from Anderlecht to the centre of Brussels. They bought, in 1616, the house of the famous Flemish anatomist Andreas Vesalius from the duchess of Bournonville and organised their monastery there. The architect De Bruyn, who had built the House of the dukes of Brabant on the Grote Markt, made plans for the church in 1700. The monastery was suppressed in 1796, and the building was used first as a hostel for beggars, then for industrial purposes, as a tobac- co factory, a military hospital and a women's prison. The church was closed in the same year. The parishioners succeeded in getting it reopened in 1818 and in 1849 the tower and upper part were restored. Its most outstanding feature is the two heavy col- umns which cover almost all the façade on huge plinths. A single entablature, supported by strong buttresses, the two columns mentioned above and the corner pillars complete the façade. The interior

A statue of St. Gorik stands above his altar in the church of the sisters of St. Clare (Rijkeklaren).

The sacristy of the church of the Rich Clares (Rijkeklaren) contains wonderful vestments and this picture.

The St. Katelijne church and the tower of the old church demolished in 1893.

has been changed. The nave is rectangular and heavy pillars support the broad arches between the centre and sides as well as the low dome. The entablature surrounds the whole building and the choir arches, the dome and the inner side of the arches are decorated with arabesques. The pulpit depicts the World, supported and surrounded by the four Evangelists: the lion (St. Mark), the ox (St. Luke), the angel (St. Matthew) and the eagle (St. John). The chapel of Our Lady of Loretto added in 1621 is worth visiting. The statue of the Virgin behind the altar is said to have been carved from the legendary oak tree which grew from the stick planted by St. Guy in Anderlecht, which leads us to speak of the St. Peter's church there. This collegiate church is one of the most remarkable in Brabant. A chapter of canons was installed there in the eleventh century in honour of St. Guy (950-1012). The church was built by the architect Mathias Keldermans in 1517 but was only completed in 1898 by van Ysendijck. The late gothic tower, and the main entrance with its arch containing statues of St. Peter and St. Guy are remarkable. Moreover it contains a late gothic parapet and a pointed window lets the light fall inside. The interior and furnishings are also attractive. High stained glass windows and two remarkable tombs decorate the choir, and the romanesque crypt (eleventh century) under the choir are some of the most important historical remains in Belgium.

The Basilica of the Sacred Heart (Basiliek van het H.

The beautiful baroque façade of the church of the beguinage, one of the beautiful in the country, is a souvenir of its former wealth.

The interior of the beguinage church is a mixture of gothic and baroque, with impressive proportions and exuberant decoration. The central part of the transept is supported by massive pillars surmounted by Corinthian capitals.

The Finisterrae church.

Hart) has been constructed on the top of the Koekelberg. The Elizabeth Park had been laid out on this "plateau" in 1880. Twenty-five years later Leopold II laid the foundation stone of the national Basilica of the Sacred Heart to commemorate the seventy-fifth year of Belgian independence. The first plan was for a gothic-style church and was by the architect Langerock of Louvain. It was too expensive and could not be continued. After the First World War in 1919 the architect Van Huffel from Ghent was given a new commission and work began again in 1926, to be continued by his successor Paul Rome after his death in 1935.

Cardinal Mercier desired that this sacred building should be the Basilica of Peace. Work continues thanks to yearly gifts by the faithful. The basilica which is the fourth largest in the world is in neo-byzantine style and has impressive proportions. The skeleton is in reinforced concrete, the walls in brick on a lower part in stone. A stainless steel cross, five metres high and weighing a thousand kilos stands on the dome. The whole building is 167 metres long, the

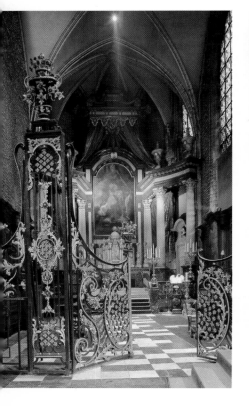

The attractive wrought iron gates of the St. Nicholas church (St.-Niklaaskerk).

The "Holy Virgin with the sleeping Child" ascribed to Rubens.

The St. Nicholas altar in Louis XIV style.

nave 107 metres, the dome 100 metres high and the towers on the façade 65 metres. The exterior has been much criticized for its lack of character but the interior has an attractive form with marble high altar and walls decorated with terracotta, attractively coloured stained glass windows by Anto Carte, Heut, Coëme, Maes, Slagmuylder, Weemaes, Colpaert and some contemporary artists. There are extremely valuable objects among the cathedral treasures.

The town hall in Brussels is undoubtedly one of Belgium's most beautiful buildings. The first stone of this gothic jewel was laid in 1402, and three years later it was completed. The only entrance used to be by

The reliquary in gilded copper, of the Gorkum Martyrs.

The Basilica of the Sacred Heart (H. Hartbasiliek) of Koekelberg.

the Lion Stairway. The lions were only added in 1770. The most beautiful sculptures of the Brabant school stand under the portico of the right wing. Both sides are decorated with sculptures of famous citizens of Brussels including the painter Barend van Orley, the poet J.B. Houwaert, the painter Roger Van der Weyden, the anatomist Andreas Vesalius, the architect-painter J. Franckaert, the painter John Bruegel the Velvet, the statesman and poet M. van St. Aldegonde, and the chronicler John De Potter.

The interior is dominated by Flemish art in the form of tapestries, paintings, painted ceilings, sculpture and carving. Paintings by John van Orley (1665-1735) and Frans Snijders hang in the staircase, as well as the bust of the Belgian statesman Frère-Orban (1812-1896) by E. Simonis. The first floor corridor is chiefly hung with portraits of rulers and princes who ruled in the Netherlands. To the right are the offices of two aldermen: one contains a sixteenth century Brussels tapestry and the other is called the Burgomasters' Room with portraits of all the burgomasters since 1830. A staircase on the left leads to the other aldermen's offices which are all richly decorated with tapestries, paintings and other artistic treasures. A passage leads on the other side to the Council Chamber, (Raadszaal) where the Estates of

The Basilica of the
Sacred Heart (H.
Hartbasiliek) is the
fourth largest basilica
in the world after St.
Peter's in Rome, St.
Paul's in London and
St. Mary's in Seville.

The Holy Sacrament
forms the theme of
the six stained glass
windows by J. Louis
in the sides of the
apse.

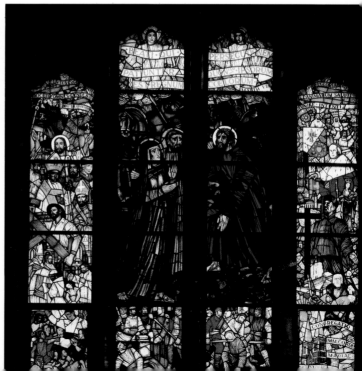

The choir of the old church of Our Lady (O.-L.-Vrouwkerk) in Laken.

The new church of Our Lady (O.-L.-Vrouwkerk) in Laken was erected by the architect Poelaert in memory of Queen Maria-Louiza.

The monument to King Leopold I in Laken.

When the
town hall in
Brussels had
only one
wing, entry
was gained
by the Lion
Staircase.

The battle between Archangel Michael, the patron saint of Brussels and the devil or dragon is often the theme of decoration inside the town hall.

One of the many beautiful tapestries decorating the walls of the town hall in Brussels.

The Maximilian Room with above the fireplace the portrait of Maximilian of Austria and Mary of Burgundy. The tapestries depict "The Life of Clovis" and were made in the Van der Borght workrooms in Brussels.

The Council Chamber of the town hall in Brussels where the council meets. The tapestries from cartoons by Victor Janssens were woven by U. Leyniers and H. Reydams. Victor Janssens painted the "Gathering of the Gods" on the ceiling.

The town used to organize great feasts and ceremonies in the Gothic Hall. Later concerts were added. The tapestries from cartoons by Willem Geets were made in the van Bracquenié workrooms; and represent the crafts and gilds of Brussels.

"De Schone Kamer" (The Beautiful Room) is panelled in Louis XIV style and is used as an alderman's office.

Brabant used to meet and where the city Council now deliberates. Victor Janssens painted the "Gathering of the Gods" on the ceiling, in which Jupiter hands the Crown to a woman who depicts the duchy of Brabant. An interesting guided tour of the town hall includes the Grangé Gallery, the Chamber of Maximilian, the Burgomaster's Office, the Gothic Hall and the Wedding Hall.

Opposite rises the lacy façade of the Broodhuis. It contains the valuable City Museum, which is particularly well-known for its collection of Brussels' pottery and porcelain, two Brussels' altar screens, the statues of the prophets which before the 1840 restoration stood above the entrance door of the town hall, and for the famous tapestry of the legend of "Our Lady op-Stocksken" (1518) one of Barend van Orley's master-pieces, and Peter Bruegel's picture "The Wedding Feast". The hall containing the altar screens, that containing the Cariatides (eighteenth century) with pictures, sketches and sculptures, the hall of the Prophets with fourtheenth, fifteenth and sixteenth century stone sculpture, St.

The Broodhuis, which houses the City Museum.

Michael's hall and the room of the craft gilds and everything pertaining to them are on the ground floor. On the first is a collection of seals from documents, medals and coins, of lace, of ceramics, of the Brabant revolution, of that of 1830 and of the French period. The Wilson room with paintings from the sixteenth, seventeenth and eighteenth centuries and Mannekenpis' room with his approximately three-hundred and fifty costumes are on the second floor.

To the left of the town hall in the Grote Markt stands the Brewers' House (Brouwershuis), which is also known as the "Golden Tree". For completeness' sake it may be added that the building was called "The Hill" in the thirteenth century. It became the gild-hall of the brewers of barley beer at the beginning of the seventeenth century, and contains today an important collection of objects illustrating this old trade. From 1765 onwards a statue of St. Arnulf, their patron saint held his protecting hand over his brewers in the attractive cellar of Spanish masonry. It is possi-

Plan of Brussels in 1748.

An imposing staircase leads to the collections of seals, lace and ceramics.

The altar-screen gallery in the Broodhuis contains the Saluces screen (early sixteenth century) of which the carved part depicts the "Life of the Virgin" and the painted part the "Life of St. Joseph". It bears the word "Bruesel".

Brussels' tapestry of 1575 depicting the legend of "Tristan and Isolde".

The Broodhuis is especially well-known for its collections of Brussels' porcelain and pottery, but the stained glass is also important.

ble to see there an ancient brewery with its wooden vats, open-hearth, shovels, buckets, pitchers and authentic filter baskets. There is an old cooper's work-shop with all its tools, near the fermenting cellar. Just next to the brewery there is a reproduction of an old inn with pitchers in pottery and porcelain, old glasses, tankards and barrels with wooden taps. The old-times' atmosphere is maintained by many details such as a ''forgotten'' overall, a picturesque pipe-rack, and the chimney with its chimney crook and iron kettle for water. Memories of yester year…

Such talk of by-gone times turns one's thoughts to a very old profession, needlework, and lace-making.

Beautiful collections of Brussels' porcelain by well-known old Brussels' firms like Monplaisir, Faber and Ghobert de St. Martin.

A complete nineteenth century brewery has been set up in the fine cellars of the Brouwershuis (Brewers' House).

Brussels' lace, especially with its "point d'Angleterre" became extraordinarily popular in the second half of the seventeenth century. It was the most popular and luxurious but most expensive of all lace. Flemish lace and especially that of Brussels was exported all over Europe, and reached its climax in the eighteenth century. The French Revolution brought about its decline and enormous fortunes could no longer be made from it as, although it continued to exist, it was on a more modest scale. Brussels' lace is still the most beautiful of all. Artists and lace-makers have started schools of lace-making which are increasingly popular with Flemish girls. A quite different star in the firmament in Brussels is called "Toone". Toone and his marionettes are an essential part of popular entertainment there, and in the picturesque "Ilôt Sacré", in the old heart of the town, the marionette theatre Toone VII, is run by José Géal. While strolling round this area full, above all, of restaurants, the visitor should keep an eye open for the alley called the Schuddeveldgang which runs into the Korte Beenhouwersstraat, where Toone lives with his family of puppets.

An impressive neo-classical building attracts attention in the Regentschapsstraat. Is was built in 1876 by the architect Balat and consists of four Corinthian columns in granite with bronze plinths bearing an entablature on which symbols of Painting, Sculpture, Architecture and Music appear. The Belgian Royal Museum of Fine Arts comprises two parts, one for old, and the other for modern art. The former is one of the richest in Europe and contains in the first place a treasure in Flemish art: of the 1.500 pictures about 1.000 Flemish and the rest foreign are divided between twelve galleries. The rare fourteenth century "Scenes from the life of Our Lady" painted on wood; works by Roger Van der Weyden, Hugo Van der

The Museum of
Costume and of Lace
is at Violetstraat 6,
near the Grote Markt.
There is a school of
lace-making on the
first floor.

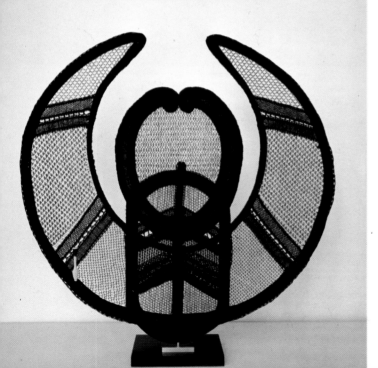

All the puppets with which the legendary puppet plays were performed from Toone I to Toone VII can be seen on the first floor of the Toone theatre in the Schuddeveldgang. The museum imitates a nineteenth century Brussels' inn.

The Koninklijke Musea voor Moderne Kunst en voor Oude Schilderkunst (The Royal Musea of Modern Art and Old Art) in the Regentschapsstraat.

Goes, Thierry Bouts, Memling, Gerard David, and Jerome Bosch from the fifteenth; of Quentin Metsijs, Barend van Orley, Peter Bruegel, Pourbus from the sixteenth and Rubens, Jordaens, Brouwer and David Teniers from the seventeenth, while foreign artists are represented by French Primitives, the Master of Moulins, Claude Lorrain, the Italians Crivelli and Guardi, and the seventeenth century Dutch of whom Frans Hals, Rembrandt, Van Goyen, Ruysdael, Hobbema and Steen, are the most remarkable. There is also a collection of about a thousand pieces of sculpture in marble, bronze and terracotta represent-

ing chiefly Belgian seventeenth, eighteenth, nineteenth and twentieth century art. The Museum of Modern Art contains the most important collection of Belgian paintings, drawings and sculpture of the last two-hundred years, although there are important foreign works by i.a. Rodin, Bourdelle, Zadkine, Moore, Chadwick, Marini, Courbet, Sisley, Gauguin, Matisse, Dufy, Vlaeminck, Vasarely and Dali. Across the road on the corner of the Regentschapsstraat and the Kleine Zavel is the Royal Academy of Music (Koninklijk Musiekconservatorium) and the Museum of ancient Musical Instruments. It contains a

The Museum of Old Art possesses some Bruegel canvases including "The Census in Bethlehem".

This painting by Eugeen Laermans (1864-1940) who struggled against the impressionists hangs in the Museum of Modern Art. He painted the tragedy of existence with a strong palet.

The Historical Museum of Musical Instruments is in the Kleine Zavel on the corner of the Regentschapsstraat. It possesses a fascinating collection of about five-thousand authentic musical instruments.

fascinating collection of about five-thousand authentic musical instruments from all periods and places. There are more than one-hundred and fifty unique examples. It is a souvenir of a forgotten glory of local cultural history when the family Ruckers of Antwerp in the sixteenth and seventeenth centuries built harpsichords copied all over the civilized world. ''Sic transit gloria mundi'' is inscribed on the lid of a spinet made by Joris Britsen in Antwerp in 1686 which is one of the most remarkable instruments in the museum. It contains also all the instruments of a complete Mozart orchestra, a series of original instruments from Venice in Monteverdi's time, flutes and oboes by the wind instrument maker Rottenburgh of Brussels and a ''Componium'' or composing machine invented in 1821 by Diederich Nicolaus Winkel. Small-scale concerts using examples from this remarkable collectlon are often organized there.

An equally important, but entirely different, building can be seen in the Sint-Gillis suburb, Amerikaansestraat 25. This is a quite exceptionally attractive house by Horta. It is a protected building of the Royal Commission of Monuments and Landscapes and is one of the most important musea in Europe. Victor Horta, the spiritual father of the ''modern style'' drew architecture about 1900 out of the cul-de-sac into which it had moved through lack of creativity and inspiration.

He was obviously entirely misunderstood and undervalued by his contemporaries. In 1893 he signed his ''Art nouveau'' manifesto by building his house in the P.E. Jansonstraat 6 for the engineer Tassel. The Brussels' weekly ''L'art moderne'' then wrote an arti-

The Victor Horta Museum in Sint-Gillis powerfully emanates the "modern style".

cle typical of the period. "It is possible, these days, to build, according to fancy, a romanesque or gothic church, or even a Flemish renaissance town hall or a neo-Greek museum. The accepted formulas are applied but the result is not a work of art because the parish or the town council must be happy about it! Because neither has the necessary taste the result is obvious. That is why extraordinary buildings, which remind us like fair-ground constructions, of glorious periods in our history, appear in our towns and re-

mind us more of wedding-cakes than of architecture. The tradition has been broken with. No progress can be made while our architects are fastened on the past. Architecture lives like speech. It expresses the period in which we live". This was also Victor Horta's belief. His originality is expressed in this house which he created and in which he lived. The National Council of the Order of Architects is now settled there. The Jubelpark and its musea are surrounded by about 60 acres of beautiful grounds, commanded by the

The dominant Arch of Triumph in the Jubelpark.

Triumphal Arch. These huge buildings which housed international exhibitions in 1880, 1888 and 1897 were planned by the architect Bordiau. The monumental entrance 45 m. in height was constructed in 1905 to plans by the architect Girault to commemorate Belgium's seventy-fifth birthday. The decoration of the arches was done by Thomas Vinçotte and the Triumphal Chariot by Julian Dillens. The whole composition depicts a triumphant Belgium looking towards the future. The Belgian provinces symbolized as gigantic figures ornament both sides of the three-arched entrance. The Triumphal Arch is connected to the two wings (of 1880) by semi-circular colonnades. The annual trade fairs of the capital were held there until 1935 when they were transferred to the exhibition hall in the Heizel park.

The Royal Military and War Museum (Koninklijk Museum van het Leger en de Krijgsgeschiedenis) and the Museum of Art and History are housed here. In 1910 a collection of army souvenirs was made on the occasion of the world exhibition. As the Museum of the Army it was exposed in the abbey of Terkameren in the former Military Academy. After the war it was installed in a part of the Jubelpark and the opening

Fine galleries bring the Antique world to life in the Royal Musea of Art and History.

ceremony in the presence of King Albert took place on July 22, 1923. One of the most impressive exhibits is an enormous painting by Bastien called "The Panorama of the IJzer" (75 m × 10 m) depicting the battles there between 1914-18. In addition there are collections from the eighteenth century to the present, of uniforms, weapons, aeroplanes, airships, models of boats, and posters and photographs of the forces in the two world wars.

The Museum of Art and History (Koninklijke Musea voor Kunst en Geschiedenis) in the Nerviërsstraat in the Jubelpark is one of the most important in Europe.

It contains i.a. a complete survey of ancient civilizations including remarkable sections on Belgian prehistory, and Ancient Asia, Greece and Rome. America, Africa and Oceania are also represented by important objects. One of the most important sections is concerned with the crafts including tapestries of the highest quality from Brussels (Barend van Orley), Tournai, France and Germany. National folklore is also depicted in its typical expression. This museum possesses an important collection of pottery and textiles (Coptic and Byzantine, Persian, Italian and French silk, embroidery from the Netherlands,

The Art Museum possesses among its very rich collection four Flemish tapestries of the "Triumph of the Virtues" of about 1515.

and Brussels' lace). An important section concerns ancient history in general where a representative collection concerns Egypt in the time of the pharaos. A series of Roman and Greek statues, beautiful Greek vases, important mosaics, and a model of Rome in the fourth century, (by Bigot) can also be examined while there are interesting collections of Moslem, and ancient Chinese ceramics.

Among the collection of arts and crafts wooden statues from the eleventh to the thirteenth centuries and a unique collection of altar screens and parts of such works from the fifteenth and sixteenth centuries must be mentioned.

A particularly valuable collection of ivories and beautiful examples of wrought iron from the Maas school (twelfth and thirteenth centuries), Limoges enamels from the thirteenth and multi-coloured and grey from the sixteenth are also represented. A chronological repertory of textiles from the beginning of our era to the nineteenth century also exists. An extensive series of tapestries depicts their history from the fifteenth to the eighteenth century, while the museum possesses one of the most important collections of lace (sixteenth-twentieth centuries) in Europe as well as ceramics and porcelain from Tournai, Brussels, France, Germany and England. The section

A royal exhibit from the Carriage Museum.

Sarcophagi and mummies are carefully preserved in the ancient history section.

The Art and History Museum is particularly proud of its collection of fifteenth and sixteenth century altar-screens.

The Royal Museum of the Army and Military History is the most well-known in the world in this field. It possesses a treasure in its collections connected with soldiers, weapons and war documents.

The Aviation Hall is one of the greatest attractions in the museum and contains i.a. a DC 3 of 1939, a Messerschmidt, a 1911 Bleriot, a Havilland Tiger Moth, a Maurice Farman, and a Hurricane from the Second World War which has been recently added a Sabena-Caravelle. The enormous canvas (photo below) 75 m. wide, and 10 m. high covering the wall is the "Panorama of the IJzer" by the painter Bastien.

The prince of humanists passed wonderful days in Swan House in the Kapittelstraat in Anderlecht with his friend canon Pieter Wychman. 22 of Erasmus' letters which have been conserved speak with affection of Brabant.

Gothic cupboards and a Brabant open-hearth decorated the room of the author of the popular "Praise of Folly".

The Erasmus house has been taken over as a museum with a library of hundreds of books of all periods about him.

The valuable jewel of Eastern art, the Chinese Pavilion, stands in the midst of a beautiful park.

The attractive rooms in Louis XIV and Louis XVI style with Chinese decorations.

One looses one's way in an Eastern palace...

devoted to scientific instruments i.a. astronomical, and the very important collection of clocks (seventeenth-nineteenth centuries) must be mentioned while the visitor interested in folklore will find an absolute treasure-trove of ex-voto's, pilgrimage pennants, popular games, signs, pictures, etchings, playing-cards, toys, dolls, baking-tins and all sorts of house-hold articles. Finally there is a carriage museum with eighteenth and nineteenth century vehicles, and illustrating the development of the bicycle and some motor vehicles.

Near St. Peter's church in Anderlecht rises the "Huys de Swaene" (Swan House) in a beautiful garden.

Erasmus lived there as a guest of his friend Peter Wychman, the owner of this gentleman's residence. The building, of 1515, is in Spanish brick in renaissance style with attractive step gables. Many objects inside, including his study, paintings, engravings, the first editions of his works, manuscripts etc. are reminders of Erasmus. The study is an airy room with ceiling and floor in wood, and portraits and documents hanging on the white walls. Gothic cupboards and a Brabant open-hearth complete it while in the corner by the window stands Erasmus' desk and his chair with the date 1518 on its back. Near the Eeuwfeestpaleizen near the "Dikke Linde" cross road

The Japanese Tower is seventy metres high!

is John of Bologna's ''Neptune'' fountain. This is a copy of the fountain made by a Flemish sculptor for the Piazza del Nettuno in Bologna in Italy. Behind it stands the Chinese Pavilion surrounded by attractive flower beds. This special jewel was commissioned by Leopold II from the French architect Marcel, and contains rooms in Louis XIV and Louis XVI style decorated with Chinese designs. Several rooms contain a rich collection of Chinese objects and it was at first intended by Leopold II to use it as a restaurant but the idea was never put into effect. The

Verhaeghe-De Nayer foundation has been housed there since 1946. It includes porcelain, silver and gold objects from China, Japan and Western Europe.

Diagonally opposite, in the Van Praetlaan stands the Japanese Tower which is an exact copy of a Japanese temple — a pagoda — which is usually built in the centre of an impressive park. This tower was first shown in the world exhibition in Paris in 1900, bought by Leopold II and re-constructed on the site once occupied by the Overheembeek windmill. This work was also carried out by the French architect Marcel in 1902-1906. The tower of five stories is 70 m. high, flanked by a Japanese pavilion, and contains many Japanese products as well as pictures and statues on the walls.

Leaving Brussels itself the next visit is to Tervuren which is well-known particularly for the Royal Central African Museum (Koninklijk Museum voor Midden-Afrika). It is an impressive building complex which·on Leopold II's request was built by the French architect Charles Girault between 1904 and 1909. It is in a neo-baroque style of four wings covering 125 m. and surrounded by an attractive French garden, with, at its centre a domed rotonda. Very varied collections from Central Africa, including ethnography, geology, flora, fauna, folklore and economy can be studied there.

It is one of Belgium's most important musea and with an average of about a quarter of a million visitors each year is one of the most popular. Its twenty or so galleries provide an overall picture of various aspects of the African continent and other overseas territories. Special attention is paid to collections such as that of the products of African agriculture, the

The most popular museum in Belgium: the Museum of Central Africa in the Tervuren park.

continent's chief economic resource; the mining of such rare materials as uranium, copper and cobalt; one of the largest collections of wood in the world; the many Belgians who have played active roles in many fields, for example, in the exploration of Central Africa, the construction of the Matadi-Leopoldstad (now Kinshasa) railway, the struggle against the slave trade, and the organization of the independent state of Congo; an interesting collection of old maps and iconographical documents concerning the growth of Africa, souvenirs of the important discoveries; metal jewelry in copper, iron and silver, decorations from organic materials such as wood, shells and feathers; in the ethnology room objects typical of the various parts of Africa are represented; a choice of esthetically pleasing statues illustrate the diverse ethnical groups of Central Africa, an area of the greatest importance in that continent; objects representing the culture of Zaïre, Northern Angola, Rwanda, Burundi and the Southern Sudan; a series of statues of which some were shown in the 1897 exhibition which had as its theme Man in the Congo (Zaïre) and the contribu-

The museum provides a virtually complete survey of the peoples, institutions and civilization of Central Africa.

Central Africa's flora and fauna are cleverly exhibited while artefacts clearly reveal the way of life there.

*Market Place -
Flower-Carpet.*

*Notre-Dame du
Sablon Church.*

*The majestic central palace of the Eeuwfeest palaces —
which is now called Tentoonstellingspark — is one of the
ten built for the 1935 World Exhibition.*

tion made there by the Belgians; some cases illustrate aspects of material culture such as harvesting, hunting, fishing, agriculture and stock-raising as well as pottery and iron working etc. Three extensive dioramas illustrate Central Africa's main biotopes: the northern savanna, the equatorial forest and the southern savanna, each with its most typical fauna; there is also a section covering reptiles, fish, various groups of insects, termites and ant-hills; four special biotopes i.e. the equatorial forests, savannas, marshes and beaches are shown with their typical bird-life; in eight dioramas appear various mammals in their natural habitat; there is an overall picture of the evolution of man in Africa as illustrated by succeeding cultures from the old Stone Age to the more recent Iron Age emphasizing the excavations undertaken by the Museum in many parts of Africa; finally a room presenting aspects of mineralogy where the minerals are presented according to their chemical composition and which is particularly interesting for the diamond mining of South Africa and Kasai. Groups of visitors can enjoy a free guided tour on appointment.

Brussels Free University has been constructed in Flemish renaissance style on the edge of the Terkamerenwood.

The Flemish students obtained their own campus, called the "Oefenplein campus", a few years ago in the Pleinlaan in Elsene.

In the Montgomery underground station hangs a painting by J.M. Folon, one-hundred and fifty m² called "Magic City".

The Eeuwfeestpaleizen were constructed in reinforced concrete built for the 1935 World Exhibition by the architect Van Neck. The bronze statues about five metres high, which top the four pillars in the façade were created from sketches by the modern artist Egied Rombaux. They depict the Railways, the Marine, Transport and Air Travel and were made by Marnix d'Haveloose, Ad. Mansart, M. Marin and E. Wijnants. The stone figures beneath symbolize Mining, Science, the Metal industry, Deep-sea fishing, the Textile industry, Agriculture, the Arts, Education and Trade and were created by F. Van Hoof, Van

Goolen, A. Courtens, G. de Vreese, M. Desmare, M. de Korte, Geo Verbanck, P. Theunis, Ghysen and E. Rombaux. The central hall is 160 m. long, 90 m. wide and 31 m. high and is spanned by a single roof supported by twelve concrete arches. Eleven palaces house more or less continuous exhibitions and trade fairs such as the Car Show, the Furniture Fair, the Food Fair and the Holiday exhibition. The eleventh palace built for the World Exhibition of 1958 by the architects R. Puttemans, G. Malcause and P. Laenen is 450 m. long and 42 m. wide. This was the site of the historical abbey farm of Ossegem which was at the

The Royal Coin-
Theatre.

The remarkable
building of "La Royale
belge" was a new
architectural
inspiration in the city.

The Claverbel building still attracts a great deal of attention.

The Cementbedrijven N.V. building in the Terhulpensesteenweg in Bosvoorde was built to plans by the architect Brodsky in 1971. It has been called "lacework with cement and gilded mirrors".

Brussels' Airport in Zaventem.

junction of Affligem and Brussels. During the nineteenth century it more or less retained its countryfied character and King Leopold II ensured that it remained whole and undivided. He gave it to the State on condition that the plans made for it were carried out, and in 1927 the town of Brussels became the owner of the 250 acre estate of Ossegem.

Near the Terkamerenwood in the Franklin Rooseveltlaan is the Free University of Brussels. It was founded by Theodore Verhaeghen on November 20, 1834 in the Gothic Room in the town hall, and between 1834 and 1842 lectures were given in the former Charles of Lorraine House. The State became owner of the building and the university had to vacate it, and

move to the buildings of the Granvelle Palace in the Stuiversstraat which have disappeared to make the north-south trunk road. There were originally, in 1843, 96 registered students, which had become 700 in 1875 and by 1923 was more than 2.000. New buildings were completed on June 23, 1930 beside the Terkamerenwood in the Solbos suburb. In Flemish renaissance style they were the work of the architect Alexis Dumont. The administration, academic hall and library occupy the central building, with in the two other buildings the Faculties of Law and of Letters. The Science Faculty is at the back, near the student hostel in the A. Buyllaan, also built by A. Dumont. Theodore Verhaeghen received his

The airport has spacious modern facilities.

rightful place on a pedestal in the forecourt. A very modern Flemish Campus has been built in the Pleinlaan in Elsene and is called the "Campus Oefenplein".

Work on the long awaited Brussels underground began in 1965 and by the year 2000 should be complete enough to allow easy communication between the outer suburbs and the centre. The stations have given modern Belgian artists the chance to show their skill.

The Rondplein at the top of the Wetstraat has been entitled Robert Schumann and so has given Brussels the chance to celebrate the great French statesman who together with Churchill and Spaak was an enthusiastic supporter of a united Europe. The latter's heart beats in the huge Berlaimont Centre. This impressive complex built on an area of about 27.000 m² in an advanced architectural style to plans by the architects Lucien de Vestel, Jean Gilson, André and Jean Polak, assisted by the engineer Joris Schmidt embodies the spirit of renewal of our era. It is in the form of an equal sided cross, twelve stories high and totalling 40 m. in height. Five-thousand five-hundred European civil servants have their offices there. It has its own underground station, railway station connecting with international lines and a park for twelve-hundred cars.

Urban development after the Second World War was rather anarchic. Whole suburbs have been demolished and skyscrapers sprang up in their stead. Brussels became the capital of Europe. Old urban limits were broken through and a new urban agglomeration including eighteen surrounding suburbs was born. The

city centre became too confined for the numerous national and international concerns. Parking space became critical and a solution was sought in the creation of new districts on the edges.

One of the examples of this new policy is the remarkable building of the Insurance company "La Royale belge" which has been built in an attractive garden in the Vorstlaan, near the Zonien Forest in the parish of Watermaal-Bosvoorde. It dates from 1970, and it is well-balanced and unobtrusive in pale colours in a frame work of oxidized copper. Claverbel draws the eye in the same way near the race-course on the edge of the Forest. To keep the area residential in character buildings there have remained low, as was the general wish.

The huge extensive airport of Zaventem, called "Brussel-Nationaal" is in the heart of Brabant and of Belgium, and forms a most important link in international air-routes. Hundreds of thousands of civil aircraft of more than forty air-lines cross Belgian airspace or land there every year. The terminal is modern with some special shops and a free tax shop, and restaurant and bar facing the runways help to while away the time. In the arrival hall near the Customs' shed is a branch of the National Tourist Board with a numerous staff of multi-lingual hostesses. They can provide all necessary information about sight-seeing, hotel reservations and themselves sell both internal and international railway tickets.

An antique market takes place on the Grote Zavel on Saturdays and Sundays. It is very popular and an important tourist attraction. The flea market draws many people to the Vossenplein every Sunday morn-

The underrated castle-museum of Gaasbeek makes an unforgettable impression on visitors.

The twelfth century fortified castle of Bouchout in the Meise nature reserve.

ing to the most popular quarter of Brussels near the Hoogstraat and the Blaasstraat called the Marollen. It is a tradition lasting from the mid-nineteenth century where all sorts of second hand goods are argued about in the picturesque dialect of Brussels. Tasty oysters and mussels can be bought all the time from stalls in the Korte Beenhouwersstraat, the Predikherenstraat and the Beenhouwersstraat which together make up the "Ilôt Sacré". For the sweet tooth there are chocolates and "speculaas". Real Brussels' lace lies for sale in many special shops round the Grote Markt while we have already described the colourful flower sellers stationed there — on Sundays there is even a bird market.

The history of Gaasbeek castle deserves a volume to itself. The unbelievably many treasures and historical documents exhibited in the unique museum yet another. To sum it up: the castle was luxuriously furnished, after having frequently been damaged, by Renesse van Warfusée. Four of its towers were burned down in 1691 by Louis XIV's army but rebuilt thanks to Louis-Alexander Schokaert, Count of Tirimont. The estate was inherited by the wealthy family Arconati-Visconti and in 1921 was donated to the Belgian State by the Marchioness Arconati.

The historical castle of Bouchout in Meise is part of a nature reserve of about 200 acres. The medieval keep dates from the twelfth century and the main tower, 22 m. high reminds the visitor of its original purpose. The ex-Empress Charlotte of Mexico, Leopold II's sister, lived there until her death in 1927 after being mad for sixty years. Beersel castle is a thirteenth century construction typical of medieval military architecture.

The mighty towers of Beersel castle.

The beautiful old abbey of Terkameren is surrounded by five garden terraces. Founded in 1201 by the abbey of Villers-la-Ville, it was already one of the richest in the country at the end of the thirteenth century. Most of the present buildings are eighteenth century although the reliquary of the Brussels' St. Boniface who died there in 1260 are conserved in the fourteenth century church. It now contains the Institute of Advanced decorative art, the Health Department and the Geographical Institute. Near by the old Duck-Pond, one of the sources of the fickle Maalbeek, slumbers. Karreveld castle in the parish of Sint-Jans-Molenbeek is near the Koekelberg Basilica. An extremely attractive farm, it was mentioned already in the thirteenth century and gradually extended over the years until it was bought in 1930 and restored in 1956. The present buildings date from the sixteenth and seventeenth centuries and form with the park an attractive complex.

The castle of Hertoginnedal, in the Vorstlaan in Bosvoorde, was built in the eighteenth century. The earlier priory of Hertoginnedal was the first in the country of Dominican nuns and undoubtedly the oldest in the whole of the Netherlands. The order was founded in 1261 by Aleidis, Duchess of Brabant, wife of Henry III. The property was given to Prince Leopold in 1931 by Baron Dietrich de Valduchesse, the penultimate owner. It was completely restored in 1956 by the State for national and international meetings.

The famous hill of the Lion of Waterloo attracts the eye on that "sad plain" as the battle-field is known. It is 45 m. high on a man-made hill, 250 m. in diameter at its base. Two-hundred and sixty steps lead to the

Terkameren abbey and its well-known Duck Pond.

The former home farm
"Het Karreveld" in St.-
Jans-Molenbeek.

The castle of
Hertoginnedal in the
Vorstlaan in
Bosvoorde.

Terkamerenwood is the entrance to the Zonien Forest. It has been owned by the town of Brussels since 1864 and adapted by the engineer Keilig. Its greenery gives townspeople lovely walks.
In May Bosvoorde becomes fairy-like in clouds of Japanese cherry blossom.
Belgian grapes are world famous. They were developed in Brabant round Hoeilaart-Overijse.
The Tommen mill in Grimbergen watches over a picturesque landscape.

The Lion of Waterloo.

top. The lion was created by the sculptor J.F. Van Geel and cast in the Cockerill factory in Seraing. It weighs twenty-eight tons and is four and a half metres long and the same in height. A "Panorama" of the battle at the moment of the French cavalry attack, by the French painter Louis Dumoulin, in the form of a circular fresco, is mounted in a near by building, while opposite is the wax-work museum of the heroes of 1815 in uniform, including Napoleon, Wellington, Blücher, the Prince of Orange, Cambronne and Ney. The provincial museum or "Ferme du Caillou",

perhaps the most important Napoleonic museum is a few miles away in Vieux-Genappe. This farm was the Emperor's head-quarters in 1815, where he passed with his staff officers the night of June 17, 1815. There are many documents and personal possessions of both Napoleon and other important figures involved in the battle.

You may ask with surprise if this too belongs to the story of Brussels itself? Yes and no! Whoever visits the whole of Brussels cannot escape an exploration of Waterloo.

Collection ALL EUROPE

#	Title	Spanish	French	English	German	Italian	Catalan	Dutch	Swedish	Portuguese	Japanese	Finnish
1	ANDORRA	•	•	•	•	•	•					
2	LISBON	•	•	•	•					•		
3	LONDON	•	•	•	•						•	
4	BRUGES	•	•	•	•			•				
5	PARIS	•	•	•	•						•	
6	MONACO	•	•	•	•							
7	VIENNA	•	•	•	•							
11	VERDUN	•	•	•	•			•				
12	THE TOWER OF LONDON	•	•	•								
13	ANTWERP	•	•	•	•							
14	WESTMINSTER ABBEY	•	•	•	•							
15	THE SPANISH RIDING SCHOOL IN VIENNA	•	•	•	•							
16	FATIMA	•	•	•	•			•				
17	WINDSOR CASTLE	•	•	•	•						•	
19	COTE D'AZUR	•	•	•	•							
22	BRUSSELS	•	•	•	•			•				
23	SCHÖNBRUNN PALACE	•	•	•	•							
24	ROUTE OF PORT WINE	•	•	•	•					•		
26	HOFBURG PALACE	•	•	•	•							
27	ALSACE	•	•	•	•							
31	MALTA											
32	PERPIGNAN		•									
33	STRASBOURG	•	•	•	•							
34	MADEIRA + PORTO SANTO	•	•	•						•		
35	CERDAGNE - CAPCIR		•			•						
36	BERLIN	•	•	•	•							

Collection ART IN SPAIN

#	Title	Spanish	French	English	German	Italian	Catalan	Dutch	Swedish	Portuguese	Japanese	Finnish
1	PALAU DE LA MUSICA CATALANA	•		•		•						
2	GAUDI	•	•	•	•	•					•	
3	PRADO MUSEUM I (Spanish Painting)	•	•	•	•	•					•	
4	PRADO MUSEUM II (Foreign Painting)	•	•	•	•	•					•	
5	MONASTERY OF GUADALUPE	•										
6	THE CASTLE OF XAVIER	•	•	•	•						•	
7	THE FINE ARTS MUSEUM OF SEVILLE	•	•	•	•	•						
8	SPANISH CASTLES	•	•	•	•							
9	THE CATHEDRALS OF SPAIN	•	•	•	•							
10	THE CATHEDRAL OF GIRONA	•	•	•	•		•					
11	GRAN TEATRO DEL LICEO	•	•	•			•					
11	EL LICEO ARDE DE NUEVO	•					•					
12	THE CATHEDRAL OF CORDOBA	•	•	•	•	•						
13	THE CATHEDRAL OF SEVILLE	•	•	•	•							
14	PICASSO	•	•	•	•	•					•	
15	REALES ALCAZARES (ROYAL PALACE OF SEVILLE)	•	•	•	•							
16	MADRID'S ROYAL PALACE	•	•	•	•							
17	ROYAL MONASTERY OF EL ESCORIAL	•	•	•	•							
18	THE WINES OF CATALONIA	•	•	•	•							
19	THE ALHAMBRA AND THE GENERALIFE	•	•	•	•	•						
20	GRANADA AND THE ALHAMBRA	•										
21	ROYAL ESTATE OF ARANJUEZ	•	•	•	•	•						
22	ROYAL ESTATE OF EL PARDO	•	•	•	•							
23	ROYAL HOUSES	•	•	•	•							
24	ROYAL PALACE OF SAN ILDEFONSO	•	•	•	•							
25	HOLLY CROSS OF THE VALLE DE LOS CAIDOS	•	•	•	•							
26	OUR LADY OF THE PILLAR OF SARAGOSSA	•	•	•								
27	TEMPLE DE LA SAGRADA FAMILIA	•	•	•	•		•					
28	POBLET ABTEI	•	•	•	•							
29	MAJORCA CATHEDRAL	•	•	•	•	•						

Collection ALL SPAIN

#	Title	Spanish	French	English	German	Italian	Catalan	Dutch	Swedish	Portuguese	Japanese	Finnish
1	ALL MADRID	•	•	•	•						•	
2	ALL BARCELONA	•	•	•	•	•					•	
3	ALL SEVILLE	•	•	•	•			•				
4	ALL MAJORCA	•	•	•	•			•				
5	ALL THE COSTA BRAVA	•	•	•	•							
6	ALL MALAGA and the Costa del Sol	•	•	•	•							
7	ALL THE CANARY ISLANDS (Gran Canaria)	•	•	•	•			•	•			
8	ALL CORDOBA	•	•	•	•					•		
9	ALL GRANADA	•	•	•	•			•				
10	ALL VALENCIA	•	•	•	•							
11	ALL TOLEDO	•	•	•	•							
12	ALL SANTIAGO	•	•	•	•							
13	ALL IBIZA and Formentera	•	•	•	•							
14	ALL CADIZ and the Costa de la Luz	•	•	•	•							
15	ALL MONTSERRAT	•	•	•	•							
16	ALL SANTANDER and Cantabria	•	•	•	•							
17	ALL THE CANARY ISLANDS II (Tenerife)	•	•	•	•			•	•			
20	ALL BURGOS	•	•	•	•							
21	ALL ALICANTE and the Costa Blanca	•	•	•	•							
22	ALL NAVARRA	•	•	•	•							
23	ALL LERIDA	•	•	•	•							
24	ALL SEGOVIA	•	•	•	•							
25	ALL SARAGOSSA	•	•	•	•							
26	ALL SALAMANCA	•	•	•	•				•			
27	ALL AVILA	•	•	•	•							
28	ALL MINORCA	•										
29	ALL SAN SEBASTIAN and Guipúzcoa	•										
30	ALL ASTURIAS	•	•	•								
31	ALL LA CORUNA and the Rías Altas	•	•	•								
32	ALL TARRAGONA	•	•	•	•							
33	ALL MURCIA	•	•	•								
34	ALL VALLADOLID	•	•	•	•							
35	ALL GIRONA	•	•	•	•							
36	ALL HUESCA	•	•									
37	ALL JAEN	•	•	•								
40	ALL CUENCA	•	•	•	•							
41	ALL LEON	•	•	•	•							
42	ALL PONTEVEDRA, VIGO and the Rías Bajas	•	•	•	•							
43	ALL RONDA	•	•	•	•	•						
44	ALL SORIA	•										
46	ALL EXTREMADURA	•										
47	ALL ANDALUSIA	•	•	•	•							
52	ALL MORELLA	•	•	•		•						

Collection ALL AMERICA

#	Title	Spanish	French	English	German	Italian	Catalan	Dutch	Swedish	Portuguese	Japanese	Finnish
1	PUERTO RICO	•		•								
2	SANTO DOMINGO	•		•								
3	QUEBEC		•	•								
4	COSTA RICA	•		•								
5	CARACAS	•		•								

Collection ALL AFRICA

#	Title	Spanish	French	English	German	Italian	Catalan	Dutch	Swedish	Portuguese	Japanese	Finnish
1	MOROCCO	•	•	•	•	•						
2	THE SOUTH OF MOROCCO	•	•	•	•	•						
3	TUNISIA		•	•	•							
4	RWANDA	•										